First Printing, May 1998
Second Printing, November 2000
Third Printing, April 2003
Fourth Printing, October 2005
4 5 6 7 8 9

Softcover
ISBN 1-56647- 136-2

Casebound
ISBN 1-56647-189-3

Mutual Publishing, LLC
1215 Center Street, Suite 210
Honolulu, Hawaii 96816
Telephone (808) 732-1709
Fax (808) 734-4094
e-mail: mutual@mutualpublishing.com
www.mutualpublishing.com

Printed in Taiwan

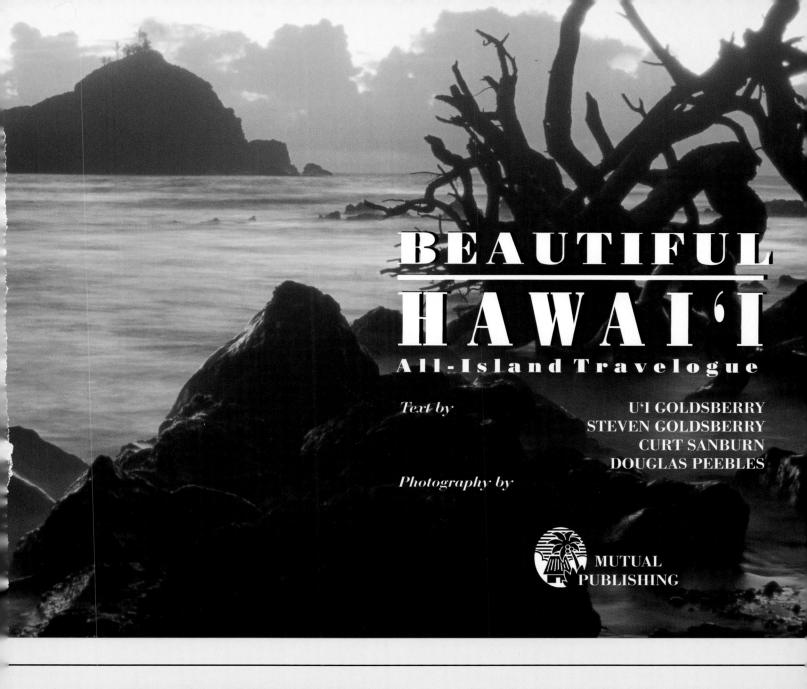

BEAUTIFUL
HAWAI'I
All-Island Travelogue

Text by

U'I GOLDSBERRY
STEVEN GOLDSBERRY
CURT SANBURN
DOUGLAS PEEBLES

Photography by

MUTUAL PUBLISHING

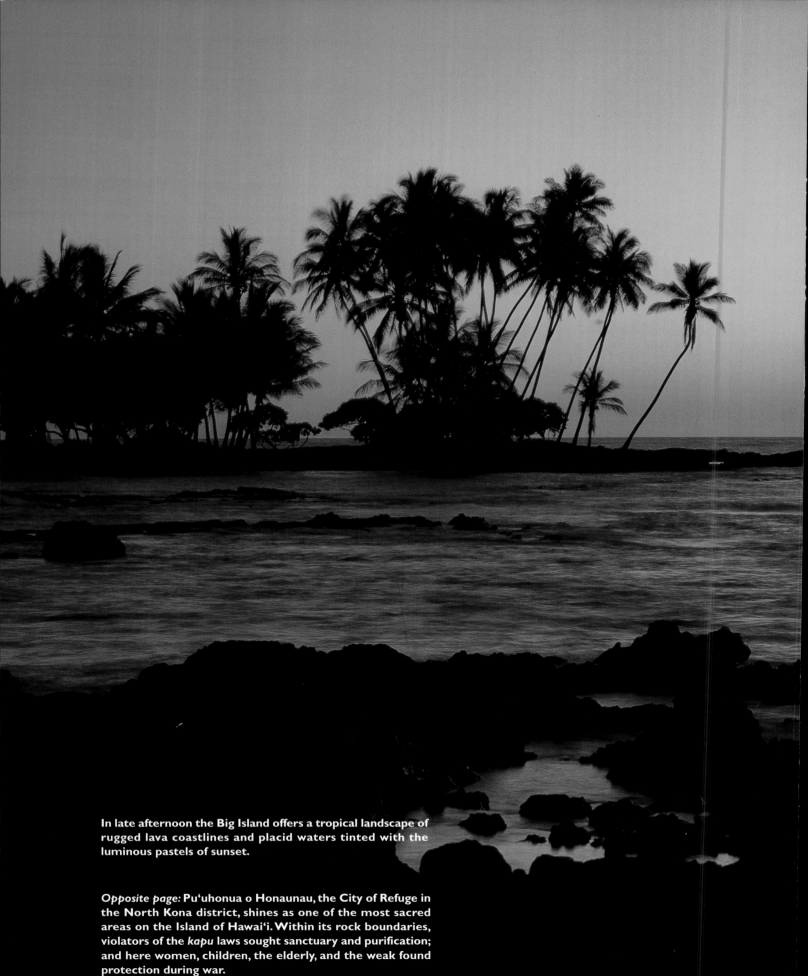

In late afternoon the Big Island offers a tropical landscape of rugged lava coastlines and placid waters tinted with the luminous pastels of sunset.

Opposite page: Puʻuhonua o Honaunau, the City of Refuge in the North Kona district, shines as one of the most sacred areas on the Island of Hawaiʻi. Within its rock boundaries, violators of the *kapu* laws sought sanctuary and purification; and here women, children, the elderly, and the weak found protection during war.

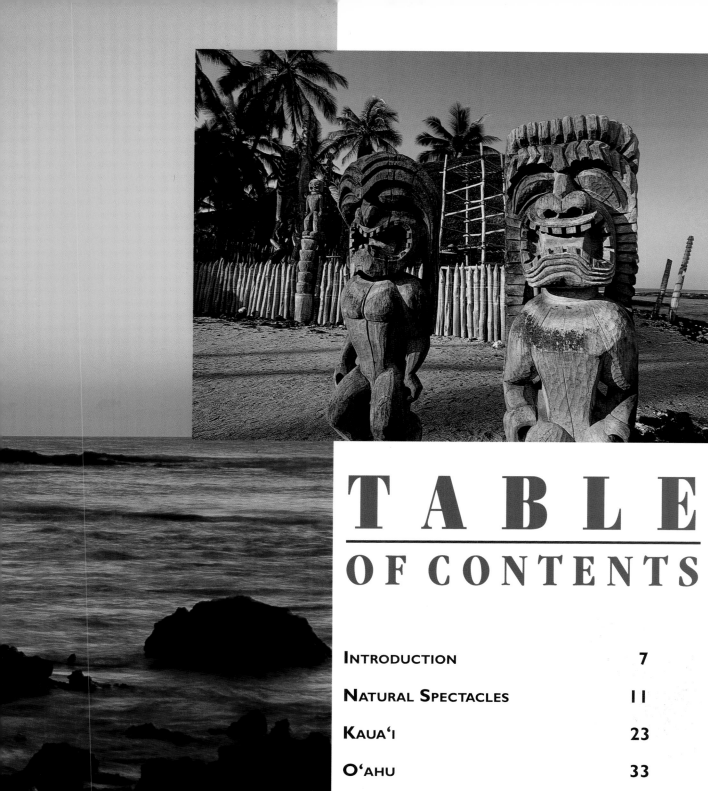

T A B L E
OF CONTENTS

3

KAUA'I

Ha'ena • • Princeville
Kalalau Valley • Hanalei • • Kilauea Point
Alaka'i Swamp • • • Kilauea
Barking Sands • Koke'e State Park • Mt. Wai'ale'ale
Waimea • Waimea Canyon • Kapa'a
Hanapepe • • Wailua
Kalaheo • Lihu'e

NI'IHAU

O'AHU

Sunset Beach • • La'ie
Hale'iwa •
Waialua •
Ka'ena Point • • Wahiawa • Chinaman's Hat
Wai'anae • • Kane'ohe
Pearl City • Aiea • Kailua
Waipahu •
Pearl Harbor • • Waimanalo
'Ewa Beach • Honolulu • Hawaii Kai
Honolulu Harbor • Waikiki Beach • Kahala • Hanauma Bay
Downtown Honolulu • Diamond Head

MOL

Kalaupapa • Kalaupa
Kaunakakai
Shipwreck Beach • Lana'
Lodge at Ko'ele • Mane

LANA'I Manele Bay Hotel Resort

THE HAWAIIAN ISLANDS

Each of Hawai'i's islands—Kaua'i, O'ahu, Moloka'i, Lana'i, Maui, Kaho'olawe, the Big Island of Hawai'i—has its own personality.

KAHO'OLA

ʻI

Historical Park

Iawa Valley

Kapalua

MAUI

Wailuku

Kahului

Lahaina

Makawao

Hana Highway

Pukalani

Kula

Kihei

Hana

Wailea

Haleakala National Park

use Bay

Kipahulu

Seven Pools

Moʻokini Heiau

Hawi

Waipiʻo Valley

Kawaihae

Honokaʻa

Waimea

Akaka Falls

Waikoloa

Rainbow Falls

Mauna Kea

Hilo

Saddle Road

Kailua-Kona

Mauna Loa

Volcano House

Park Headquarters

Keahakeua

Volcano

Captain Cook

Hawaii Volcanoes

Puʻu oʻo Crater

National Park

Kalapana

Kaʻu Desert

HAWAIʻI

Ka Lae

(South Point)

Princeville, a resort development near the town of Hanalei on the island of Kaua'i, exudes a tropical tranquillity unrivaled among Hawai'i's hotels. Tiny cove-like beaches of white sand and shimmering aqua-blue water dot the coastline of this, the northernmost tourist destination in Hawai'i

INTRODUCTION

Situated almost dead-center in the middle of the Pacific Ocean, in the relentless surge of wind-tossed waves, lies the most remote land form on earth—the fragmented arc of high islands called Hawai'i. Towering shield volcanoes, now eroded and gullied, comprise the emerald green mountains of this ancient archipelago.

Of the eight major islands, four stand out as the most dramatic and alluring, and not coincidentally the most heavily populated—Kaua'i, O'ahu, Maui, and Hawai'i (The Big Island).

Kaua'i is the oldest of the group at roughly 5 million years—five or six times as old as Hawai'i, at the opposite end of the chain. Frequent rains (Kaua'i's Mount Wai'ale'ale is the wettest spot on our planet) have eroded the island into broad alluvial plains and deep canyons cut by Hawai'i's only true rivers.

Kaua'i's erosion has had its artistic effect in the forms of steep pinnacles and razorback ridges, remnant mountains draped in velvety folds, gorges whose rock walls reveal millions of years of multi-hued geology, and countless dream-like waterfalls.

Sixty miles to the southeast, across a treacherous channel, lies the island of O'ahu, where Polynesia meets the twenty-first century. Nowhere in Hawai'i

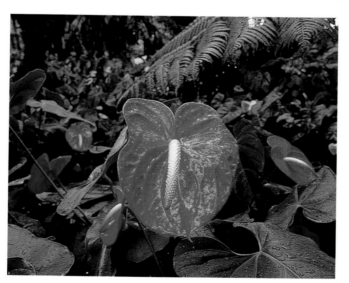

The original anthuriums were brought to Hawai'i by an English missionary, Samuel Damon, in 1889 from Colombia, via London. The "Bright Reds" range in size from tiny (peewees) to extra long, and account for almost half of Hawai'i's exotic flower sales.

are the contemporary realities and complexities of life in paradise more vivid with the booming prosperity, the cultural and racial confluences, the proud history, the trade-offs between preservation and progress played out against a spectacular natural beauty.

The simplest images express it best: Honolulu's glittering high-rises crowded between blue sea and green mountains; freeway traffic cooled by trade winds and gilded by blazing sunsets; the stunning regularity of rainbows arched over the city and its outlying plains.

Honolulu and Waikiki usually overwhelm any other impression of the island. However, the great surprise to most visitors is how spectacular the rest of O'ahu is both physically and socially.

Topographically, this 600-square-mile, mature volcanic island is the most varied and intimate of the major Hawaiian Islands. Spread out along O'ahu's four distinct coastlines like a checklist of tropical essentials are coral reefs, sheltered lagoons, scores of beaches, well-defined bays, view-perfect promontories, mist-shrouded valleys, dry leeward plains, and sheer, fluted cliffs.

Although O'ahu has ultra-famous Waikiki, arguably the best known island is Maui. Its name is derived from the mischievous Polynesian demigod,

Water from the frequent rains that wash the lush green volcanic peaks of the Hawaiian Islands collect into streams, then cascade in pluming waterfalls to plunge pools. The steep cliffs around the falls drip with a gorgeous display of tropical flora: *kukui, lo'ulu* palms, *ti,* heliconias, gingers, African tulips, and *hala.*

Maui, who stole the secret of fire from the gods and slowed the sun's flight across the sky so Hawaiian days would be longer and warmer.

Like its namesake, the island of Maui revels in the sun and devotes its long days to playful and athletic pleasures. It is the most glamorous and flamboyant of all the Hawaiian Islands. With miles of swimming beaches, two perpetually sunny coasts, awesome mountains, and calm, leeward seaways ringed by a majestic fleet of lesser islands, Maui has every right to its stellar reputation, international charm, and the phrase used to describe it: *"Maui no ka 'oi,"* Maui is the best!

The second youngest and the second largest of the islands, Maui includes in its 728 square miles two distinct volcanic domes—mighty Haleakala ("House of the Sun") and the compact West Maui Mountains. The two eroded volcanoes are joined by Maui's central isthmus, formed a million years ago when lava from Haleakala met the shores of West Maui. The isthmus functions as a valley between the peaks—thus, Maui's nickname: "the Valley Isle."

The island of Hawai'i, commonly called "the Big Island," has only a smattering of man-made environs spread across 4,034 square miles of lava, scrub, and forested mountains. Nature looms large on this island, and nothing else compares.

The Big Island's two major shield volcanoes, Mauna Kea and Mauna Loa, climb almost 14,000 feet above the Pacific. Their wide slopes join the peaks of three smaller volcanoes on the island's perimeter: Kohala, Hualalai, and Kilauea (the most active one). Northeast trade winds stream across the young landscape, dropping moisture on the windward rain forests, funneling through the saddle areas, accelerating down the leeward declines, and eddying around Mauna Loa's buxom mass.

The Big Island's growth is measured in decades, not millennia. Within the last 200 years, over a hundred eruptions have pushed lava into various precincts across the island's southern half. At times, the molten rivers inundate towns and beaches, and they vanish. New land appears, new little cinder cones, new beaches.

After a century of ranching, fishing, and agriculture, the Big Island has become an international curiosity—the home of an active, drive-in volcano, and mega-hotels built on lava rocks at the edges of idyllic, jewel-like coastlines.

Each island possesses a unique identity, and however you imagine paradise, you're sure to find it just around the bend.

Use this travelogue as an introduction to the treasures of Hawai'i, from its natural spectacles, through its history, to its cherished activities and attractions. Only the highlights are noted here, for busy travelers whose time won't allow for deep exploration. If you want more detailed portraits of Kaua'i, O'ahu, Maui, and the Big Island, refer to the individual island titles in the series.

'Aha'i la i ka pupuhi—Travel with the speed of wind.

Liquid lava trickles in luminescent streams over the cooled lava from an older Kilauea Volcano eruption. The islands of Hawai'i were formed by this "layer upon layer" process of volcanic creation.

NATURAL
SPECTACLES

Each Hawaiian island vibrates with certain individual energies. Kaua'i, the Garden Isle, whose dormant volcano now erupts with vegetation, glistens with rainwater and the misty spindrift of scouring winter surf. O'ahu, the Gathering Place, is abustle with urban excitement and girdled by more golden beaches than you'll find along any other shore. The Valley Isle, Maui, moves to the pace of ranch-life, resorts, and remote hideaways. And Hawai'i, the Big Island, lives up to its namesake with gigantic, active volcanoes, the most extravagant hotels, and mile upon mile of startlingly unusual scenery.

Created in sequence by a slow, steady northwestward drift of a tectonic plate over a volcanic "hot spot" deep in the Pacific, these islands display astounding differences of geology and landscape, structure and grace. The process that created this archipelago began 70 million years ago with the creation of what is now the Meiji Seamount, and continues today on the Big Island at the southeastern end.

The typical young land form of the Hawaiian Islands is a rounded "shield" volcano, built by innumerable thin lava flows. Mauna Loa on the Big Island is a classic—and still active—shield volcano, rising gently to its 13,800-foot height above the crashing waves of the Pacific.

On the major islands it's easy to see the geological evolution from the swelling shapes of intact young shield volcanoes on the Big Island and Maui to the heavily eroded, jagged topography of Kaua'i. Islands to the north shrink steadily from oceanic rocks to atolls, and beyond the last dry land of Kure Atoll there are hundreds of miles of seamounts leading at last to Meiji, the first island of this ancient chain.

As you tour the Islands, and peruse these pages, take a moment to imagine the geological history of the images before you, how stubborn sea cliffs were once a molten flow of dense basalt, how a plain has been created over centuries of stream runoff, and intermittent waterfalls have grooved a precipice, how reefs have bloomed over wave-cooled lava, and how a cinder cone crater has collapsed to form a bay. Like no other such limited geographical area, Hawai'i displays the phoenix power of the earth's unending cycles of change.

A golden path of fading sunlight bestows its blessing of romance to a tropical paradise. Such soothing displays of idyllic beauty contrast the jagged coastlines, volcanic peaks, and raw, elemental forces of the Hawaiian Islands.

Ke'e cliff, just west of Ha'ena on the island of Kaua'i, is closely connected to the Pele legends. After Lohi'au died of love for Pele, his body was sequestered in a cave on this cliff. Hi'iaka and her companion, Wahine-oma'o (green woman), climbed the cliff, and with herbs and long prayers Hi'iaka restored Lohi'au to life. Three rainbows appeared, and the legendary characters slid down the rainbows to earth.

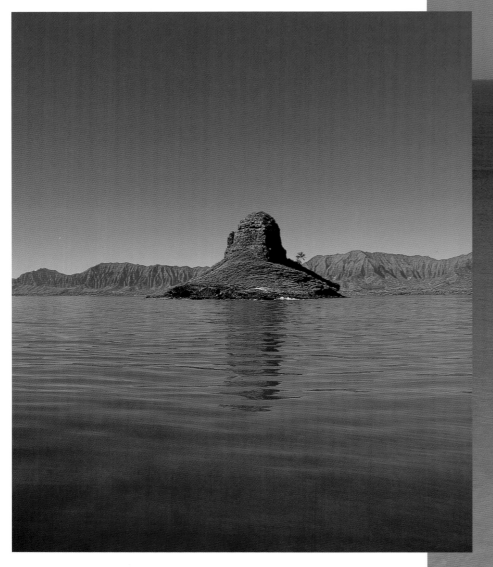

Chinaman's Hat (Mokoli'i) floats between a tranquil sea and morning sky ablaze with orange, deep purple, pink, and lavender light. Such days of calm clarity are rare on the windward coast of O'ahu: almost the entire southern half of the Ko'olau range stretches as far as the eye can see. The mountains are usually shrouded in rain clouds. Looking toward He'eia, this angle of Mokoli'i Island argues strongly for its modern name—Chinaman's Hat.

16

It's hard to see why on this calm afternoon, but when wave swells hit this coast, Makapu'u Beach becomes one of the premier bodysurfing spots on O'ahu. The rough currents of the Ka'iwi Channel between O'ahu and Moloka'i wrap around Makapu'u cliff, creating ideal conditions for wave riding.

A shroud of misty clouds drifts through the rain forests in Hawai'i Volcanoes National Park. Black-barked 'ohi'a trees tower over a blanket of *hapu'u* and '*ama'u* ferns that cover the forest floor.

The lacey fronds of the *hapu'u*, or tree fern, form the low canopy of ground cover in the rain forests of the Hawai'i Volcanoes National Park. Their shade holds the moisture close to the rocky soil, allowing splendid mosses to grow.

The beauty of Lumahaʻi Beach, near Hanalei on the island of Kauaʻi, was called Nurses' Beach in the 1958 movie musical, *South Pacific*. Breadfruit trees that once lined the shore were said to have been planted by a *menehune* named Weli.

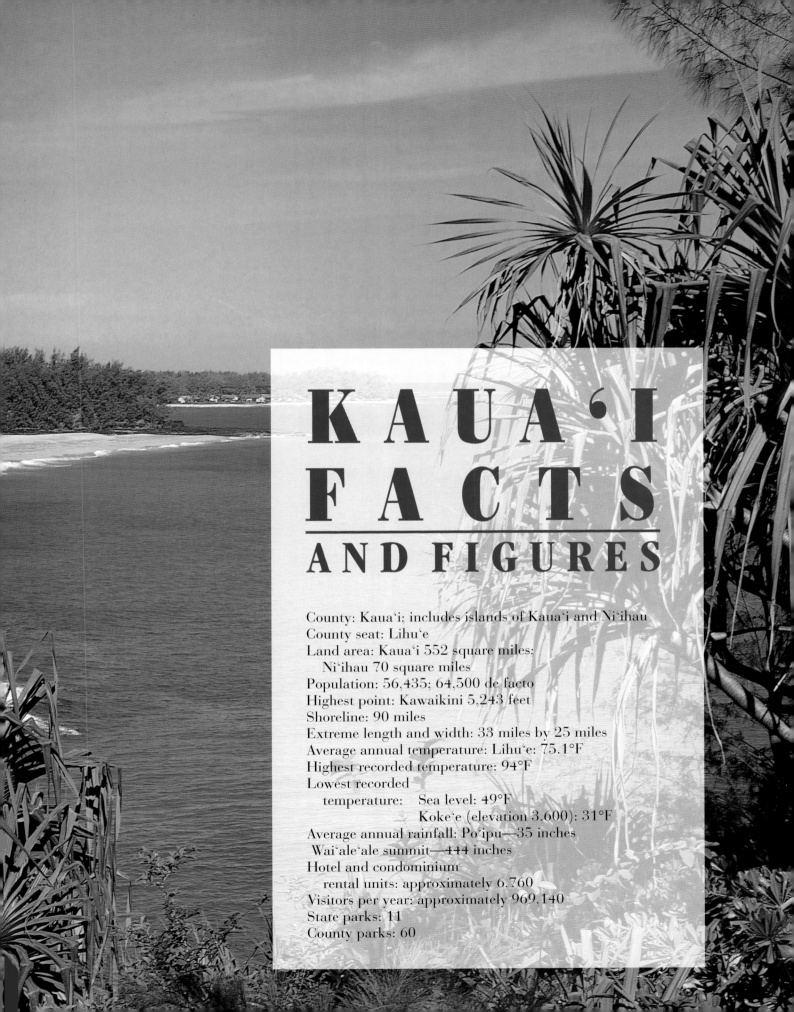

KAUA'I
FACTS
AND FIGURES

County: Kaua'i; includes islands of Kaua'i and Ni'ihau
County seat: Lihu'e
Land area: Kaua'i 552 square miles;
    Ni'ihau 70 square miles
Population: 56,435; 64,500 de facto
Highest point: Kawaikini 5,243 feet
Shoreline: 90 miles
Extreme length and width: 33 miles by 25 miles
Average annual temperature: Lihu'e: 75.1°F
Highest recorded temperature: 94°F
Lowest recorded
    temperature: Sea level: 49°F
                    Koke'e (elevation 3,600): 31°F
Average annual rainfall: Po'ipu—35 inches
    Wai'ale'ale summit—444 inches
Hotel and condominium
    rental units: approximately 6,760
Visitors per year: approximately 969,140
State parks: 11
County parks: 60

The sharply furrowed mountains of the Napali Coast, eroded by the pounding rains that frequent this island, stand as natural ramparts protecting the inland areas of Kaua'i. Campers are required to obtain permits before making the long, switch-back hike along the coast to the campsites in this state park and forest reserve.

KAUA'I

Kaua'i stands to this day as a place apart. One most days, the sixty mile Ka'ie'iewaho or Kaua'i Channel is wide enough that Kaua'i and its nearest neighbor, O'ahu, are out of sight of each other. Canoe paddlers in ancient days had to know their course between these islands because often at mid-channel neither island is visible. Kaua'i remained independent for fifteen years after Kamehameha the Great in 1795 completed his conquests of the Big Island, Maui, Moloka'i, Lana'i, and O'ahu.

Archaeologists have found on Kaua'i mysterious stone work and implements never seen on the other Hawaiian Islands. Ancient Kaua'i and neighboring Ni'ihau had their own dialect of the Hawaiian language, using "t" and "r," in words where the windward islanders used "k" and "l." More than any other island, Kaua'i is steeped in lively storytelling, legends, and myths. Every rock, peak, and cave has ancient significance; gods and ghosts animate the remote beaches.

Kaua'i is the oldest Hawaiian island at roughly five million years of age, five or six times as old as Hawai'i, the tallest and youngest of the islands, at the other end of the island chain. Heavy rains delivered by the northeast trade winds have eroded the island. Its alluvial plains are thick and rich, and its river valleys cut deep into the heart of the circular island's volcanic core.

The ancient Hawaiians may have been aware that their island would someday disappear. Legend says that a rock pinnacle at Ha'ena on Kaua'i's north shore will stand as long as Kaua'i does. When the rock falls, the island will crumble. This is the succession of geological events for Hawaiian islands: first an island, then a rock, then an atoll, and finally a shoal, of concern only to ships' navigators.

But Kaua'i's erosion has its positive side effects. One of Kaua'i's chief attractions is the drama of the wind- and water-carved landscape. Deep iron-hued canyons, tall pinnacles and dragon-teeth ridges, breathtaking sea cliffs spilling waterfalls, corrugated mountainsides like green drapery hung from the cloudy heavens—these are Kaua'i's treasures.

When the British explorer Captain James Cook landed at Waimea in January 1778, the taro farmers and fishermen of west Kaua'i thought his ships were floating islands covered with tall trees. They flung themselves to the ground when he or his men approached. They gave him water, pigs, bananas, yams, and fish—everything he wanted. In

Waimea Valley, Cook noted the neat geometry of the fields and the complex irrigation system. Expedition artist John Webber sketched the native *heiau* (temples) with their stone platforms, wooden towers, and grimacing idols.

Across the island at Wailua, the island's *ali'i* (chiefs) and *kahuna* (priests) knew nothing of the momentous events in Waimea. They carried on as usual. They gathered taxes of food from the *maka'ainana* (commoners), feasted, played games, surfed, punished *kapu* (law) violators, had children, and managed their vast estates. Their history was preserved in hours-long chants memorized by skilled court chanters who freely mixed history, legend, and fantasy.

The chants told stories of giant warriors and petulant goddesses, of great ancestors and of creation itself (as in the famed creation chant called the *Kumulipo*); stories of voyages to and from Tahiti and the Marquesan islands; and marvelous tales of the *menehune*, a legendary race of spry mountain people who built huge walls, ditches, *heiau*, and fishponds in the dark of night.

Anthropologists now say that there is no evidence that the *menehune* ever really existed. The legend they believe, recalls the earliest Marquesan settlers on Kaua'i who were subsequently ruled by the later-arriving Tahitians. The scientists have yet to explain adequately the unique "menehune" stonework and engineering feats of ancient Kaua'i.

The legends remind everyone that there is more to Kaua'i's landscape than erosion. Stones are still piled in simple terraces where gods once danced. A sleeping giant dreams on a hilltop, while below him, in Kapa'a, families shop for frozen food. At Ha'ena, two stones are thought to be two legendary brothers who came ashore to die after a long sea voyage. Their sister is a rock out on the reef, visible at low tide.

Though its erosion continues unabated, Kaua'i remains a vibrant, formidable island. It urges you to listen to its stories and understand its past. In doing so, it asks you to protect its future so that the life of the island, the murmuring mysteries of its ancient valleys and cloud-shrouded mountains, will never erode.

A traveler wrote fifty years ago: ". . . most of all, Kaua'i remains in my memory an island of fable, so near its own myths that they materialize out of its rocks and hills and live in its shifting light."

Mount Wai'ale'ale, the second highest peak on Kaua'i (5,080 feet), has an average rainfall of over 476 inches. Its Hawaiian name is quite appropriate. Wai'ale'ale means "rippling water or overflowing."

Zodiac tour boats scour the calm summer surf of Napali Coast. During the winter, open ocean waves of up to 30 feet slam into the coast, exploding into clouds of feathery spindrift.

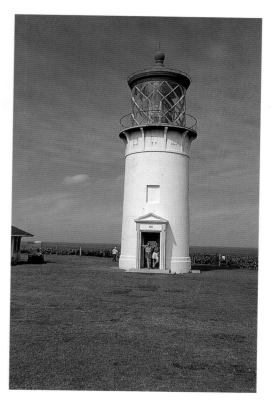

The 52-foot Kilauea Lighthouse, built in 1913, once guided ships from the Orient past Kaua'i and on to O'ahu. Poised two hundred feet above the Pacific on the tip of the Kilauea Peninsula, this weathered old beacon no longer flashes.

Hanalei means "crescent" in Hawaiian. This bay is the largest on Kaua'i, the scene of yacht racing during the summer and world-class surfing in the winter.

Limahuli Gardens, on 1,000 acres in Limahuli Valley, is a lush sanctuary for many rare and native Hawaiian plant species, as well as introduced tropicals that love the very wet conditions.

Following a heavy rain, two or three main streams cascade down the 80-foot drop of Wailua Falls.

Sun-tinged clouds, golden sand, ancient palms... a secret beach

To hike the Na Pali Coast you must follow the narrow, winding, switch-backs of the Kalalau Trail.

Waimea Canyon, known as the Grand Canyon of the Pacific, is a 3,600-foot-deep chasm carved by Waimea River and Kaua'i's frequent torrential rains.

An endangered Hawaiian Green Sea Turtle rides a wave surge over the reefs off Kaua'i's southern coast.

A bicyclist stands at Waimea Canyon lookout facing the rising sun.

It is still possible to take late afternoon runs along the secluded beaches at Princeville.

During the summer, when the water off the **Na Pali Coast** is placid and blue, **Spinner** and **Bottlenose** dolphins race and weave in front of zodiac tour boats.

The beach at Po'ipu was a sunny haven for ancient Hawaiian chiefs and today is a popular resort destination.

The lacy, green canopy of the Fern Grotto, at the head of the Wailua River and just south of Wailua Falls, is a favorite spot for romantic tropical weddings.

This panoramic view of the windward coast of Oʻahu from Kaneʻohe to Kualoa shows the classic fluted ridges and dramatic pinnacles of the Koʻolau mountain range. To the right in the photo, sitting in the waters of Kaneʻohe Bay like an afterthought of land, is Mokoliʻi Islet. In legend, Hiʻiaka, goddess of the forests, journeyed north through the island chain to fetch a young man named Lohiʻau from his home on Kauaʻi. At Kualoa, on the island of Oʻahu, she was attacked by Mokoliʻi, a huge evil lizard. During the battle, she cut off his tail and tossed it into the sea. The tail became that islet, known today as Chinaman's Hat.

O'AHU
FACTS
AND FIGURES

County: City and County of Honolulu

Land area: 597 square miles

Population: 871,766 residents; de facto, 919,200

Highest point: Mt. Ka'ala, 4,003 feet

Shoreline: 112 miles

Extreme length and width: 44 miles by 30 miles

Average annual temperature: 78.5°F

Highest recorded temperature: 94°F

Lowest recorded temperature: 53°F

Average annual rainfall at Honolulu Airport: 23 inches

Average annual rainfall: Manoa Valley 158 inches

Hotel and condominium rental units: 36,146

Visitors per year: 4,981,820

State parks: 33

County parks: 266

The coastline from Ala Moana to Waikiki. The three stretches of white sand are Ala Moana Beach (bottom), Magic Island (center), and Waikiki. The long, flat concrete slab to the left is the Ala Moana Shopping Center, once the largest shopping mall in the United States. The Ala Wai Yacht Harbor marks the entrance to Waikiki, and like a green oasis in the middle of towering high rises is the Ala Wai Municipal Golf Course. Knife-edge ridges and plunging cliffs define Na Pali.

O'AHU

Welcome to the island of O'ahu, the urban stronghold of Hawai'i's far-flung island kingdom. With a population just cresting one million, O'ahu supports nearly 80 percent of the state's residents, and entertains more tourists than all the other islands combined. But while the sprawling metropolis of modern Honolulu/Waikiki reaches skyward with its concrete and steel high-rises, the stunning natural beauties of the island remain, from the rain-catching green of the Ko'olau Mountains behind the city to the remote beaches, bays, and windswept points in "the country."

O'ahu is a wealth of contrasts. There are jammed freeways (with 5 cars for every 6 people, the island endures the most automobile-dense society on earth), but also there are rainbows rising through the valley mists beyond the traffic. Linked by O'ahu's busy roads you find neighborhoods as distinct and varied as the races living here. Many old-time Japanese families have settled in Mo'ili'ili and Kaimuki, the Caucasians east of Diamond Head, Filipinos and Samoans in Kalihi, the Chinese in Chinatown. There is much ethnic and class mixing, however. A Buddhist temple sits a block away from a Mexican restaurant. A Japanese language school shares a building with a Portuguese bakery.

And the roads take you out of Honolulu's 25-mile long urban corridor on the South Shore into the farms and plantations in the verdant heart of the island, and on to the North Shore and its wilderness of waves and rugged coast. In twenty minutes the complications of the big-city rush give way to the serenity of sun and surf.

The long Ko'olau mountain range to the east and the Wai'anae range to the west, with a broad central plain in between, define the island. The 4,000-foot peaks, sloping ridges and steep-walled *pali* (cliffs) are the remains of the much higher Ko'olau and Wai'anae volcanoes that emerged from the Pacific about three million years ago. On O'ahu, nature has had plenty of time to rearrange its crude volcanoes into a magical landscape. Eons of stream and wave erosion have carried much of the original mass back into the sea, leaving behind the soft, deeply folded draperies of Windward O'ahu and the alternating valleys and ridges that provide Honolulu's dramatic backdrop. Later volcanic activity added the finishing touch with a series of volcanic cones: the beloved landmarks of Diamond Head, Punchbowl, and Koko Head.

O'ahu has been known as "the gathering place" since ancient days, when chiefs from the other, more populous islands conferred at Waikiki, which was then neutral ground.

O'ahu's modern history begins in late 1794, sixteen years after British Captain James Cook found and named the Sandwich Islands, when a British fur trading ship, *Jackal* , inched through a break in the coral reef protecting a small O'ahu fishing village called Kou and found a commodious harbor that the sailors named Fair Haven—"Honolulu" in Hawaiian. The promise of a safe anchorage and nearby fresh water and food (and, no doubt, its exotic name) drew adventurers, sandalwood traders, merchants, and whalers from America and Europe to Honolulu. New England Protestant missionaries quickly followed—to remind the sailors away from home of their spiritual responsibilities, and to clothe and convert the Hawaiians. By 1850, when King Kamehameha III relocated the royal capital here from Lahaina, Maui, Honolulu was a bustling Pacific port-of-call.

As the city grew, its wealthy residents sought refuge from the dust, heat, and overdressed fussiness of Victorian Honolulu. They found it two miles away at Waikiki, a traditional surfing and fishing beach reserved for O'ahu's *ali'i*. Hawai'i's royalty built modest cottages there, in the ancient coconut groves at Helumoa, where the Royal Hawaiian Hotel now stands. Western businessmen followed and soon learned from the Hawaiians how to surf the gentle waves. In 1901, the Moana—a large modern hotel that rose higher than the coconut palms—opened with 100 visiting Shriners as its first guests.

Honolulu is the state capital, by far its largest city, and the headquarters for banking, construction, transportation, agriculture, manufacturing, and tourism. The U.S. Army, Navy, and Air Force commands based on O'ahu involve more than 116,000 military personnel and their dependents, and control one quarter of O'ahu's land area.

The City and County of Honolulu—a single political entity—covers the entire island; "Honolulu" usually refers to the urban swath along O'ahu's south shore from Koko Head in the east to Pearl Harbor in the west, and from the ocean into the Ko'olau

Mountains. Having their own distinct personalities are the bedroom communities of Kailua and Kane'ohe on the far side of the Ko'olau mountains; the sprawling commuter suburbs of 'Aiea, Pearl City, Waipahu, 'Ewa, and Mililani to the west; the military centers at Pearl Harbor, Hickam Air Force Base, Kane'ohe Corp Base Headquarters, Wheeler Air Force Base, and the U.S. Army Schofield Barracks; and the rural coastal communities of Wai'anae, Waialua, Hale'iwa, Kahuku, La'ie, Kahalu'u and Waimanalo.

Slightly more than half of the people on O'ahu were born in Hawai'i and call themselves kama'aina , children of the land. The rest, malihini , moved here. Thirty-three percent of the total population is Caucasian or *haole*. Another 21 percent is first-, second-, third-, or fourth-generation Japanese: *issei, nisei, sansei*, or *yonsei*. Hawaiians or part-Hawaiians constitute 18 percent. The remaining 28 percent includes Filipinos, Chinese, Portuguese, Samoans, Koreans, Tongans, Vietnamese, Cambodians, African-Americans, and Puerto Ricans, in that order of significance. Nearly half of O'ahu's marriages are interracial.

Surfers at Waimea Bay race the cresting power of the North Shore's winter surf. Riding the mountainous waves of Waimea Bay is the ultimate test of a waterman's courage, and the greatest thrill in sports.

This colorblindness, this hospitality, is the legacy of the Hawaiian people. From the moment of first contact with Europeans in 1778, the Hawaiians were open-armed. Tragically, the cost of aloha was devastating, as introduced diseases, economic exploitation, and political conquest brought the Hawaiians to the edge of extinction.

Somehow the spirit of aloha prevailed, and the Hawaiian host-culture is still the touchstone for almost every aspect of Hawai'i's uniqueness: the racial harmony, graceful way of life, famous music and dance, colorful integration of nature into man-made things, and stewardship of the 'aina, the land.

Despite intensive land and golf developments, O'ahu's pleasures are the same today as yesterday. The trade winds continue to blow and the pure colors of the mountains and the sea continue to amaze. Honolulu is still, by any measure, a glamorous, glorious city. Every day its golden people prove the remarkable durability of the aloha spirit, that guileless local friendliness that transcends the realities of the late 20th century.

Hanauma Bay was formed when the seaward wall of an ancient volcano crater collapsed. Aptly named, hanauma means "curved bay."

The pyramidal peak of Puʻuʻohulehule looks down upon Kualoa Regional Park and Hokuleʻa Beach, the site of many landings of ancient voyaging canoes.

The Polynesian Cultural Center in the small windward town of Laʻie is staffed by Polynesian and mainland U.S. students attending Brigham Young University-Hawaiʻi campus.

Hula dancers at Waimea Falls Park provide daily cultural education and demonstrations of Hawaiian dance and martial arts.

A glimpse of the sparkling skyline of Honolulu's high rises beyond the grooved green of the Koʻolau Mountains.

Towering above the central plains of Oʻahu, and stretching from Kaʻena Point to ʻEwa, the Waiʻanae Mountains are what remains of the older of two volcanoes that created the island. Kolekole Pass, the hallow declivity in this range, marks the flight path Japanese "zeros" used in their attack on Pearl Harbor.

Sunset gold silhouettes the coconut palms at Ala Moana Beach Park.

Lanikai Beach, one of the highest-priced neighborhoods on the windward coast, is known for its two offshore islands, the Mokuluas. Once an ancient fishing spot, this mile-long bay of calm water is great for swimming and kayaking.

The light of early morning glints over the foot of Diamond Head as another glorious day in paradise begins.

Colorful spinnakers plume as the weekly Friday yacht races begin from the entrance to the Ala Wai Yacht Harbor.

'Iolani Palace was built in 1882 by King David Kalakaua and Queen Kapi'olani during the twilight years of the Hawaiian monarchy.

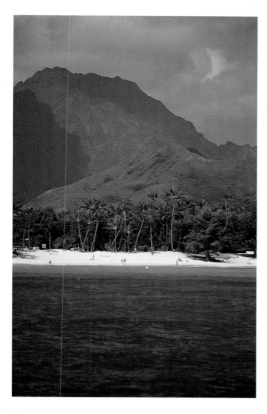

The colors of the sea at Kailua Beach Park are as extraordinary as the quality of the fine golden sand.

The Nu'uanu Pali Lookout affords a very convenient view of the corrugated ridges of the Ko'olau Mountains.

Once a wonderland of coral gardens, Kane'ohe Bay is making a strong comeback from siltation due to over-development.

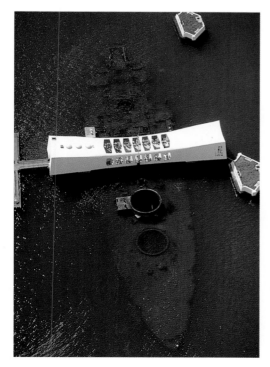

The *Arizona* Memorial shrine straddles the ghostly hulk of the **USS** *Arizona*.

The gentle breezes and lake-flat waters of Kailua Beach are perfect for Outrigger Canoe sailing.

The Kodak Hula Show, an exhibition of classical Hawaiian and Polynesian music and dance, is performed every week on Tuesday, Wednesday, and Thursday mornings at 10:00 am at the Waikiki Shell.

The upper floors of the Sheraton Waikiki Hotel offer this view of Diamond Head and the white, crescent beach of Waikiki.

The Ala Wai Yacht Harbor, at the mouth of the Ala Wai Canal, provides mooring for pleasure craft from around the world.

Hawai'i's young women of every nationality train and participate in hula demonstrations and celebrations like the Aloha Festival.

During the summer months, the sun sets into the water off of Waikiki Beach.

The classic harbor landmark, Aloha Tower, greeted seafaring visitors and merchants coming to Honolulu. Today, the newly renovated Aloha Tower hosts an upscale marketplace.

Kuka'ilimoku, Kamehameha the Great's war god, is exhibited in a sealed glass case at the Bishop Museum main gallery.

Hawaiian masons cut 14,000 large coral blocks to build Kawaiaha'o Congregational Church between 1830 and 1840.

Serving the best Chinese food to Honolulu residents since 1882, Wo Fat's Chop Suey Restaurant in Chinatown is an important historical, cultural, and sentimental landmark.

Punchbowl Crater, once known as Puowaina, or "the hill of placing (sacrifices)," today serves as the home of the National Memorial Cemetery of the Pacific.

A 45-minute jeep ride over unimproved roads transports visitors from the tropical scenery of the Saddle Road to the high-mountain snows of Mauna Kea. The summit of this great mountain offers the remarkably thin, clear air that astronomers find ideal for star-gazing.

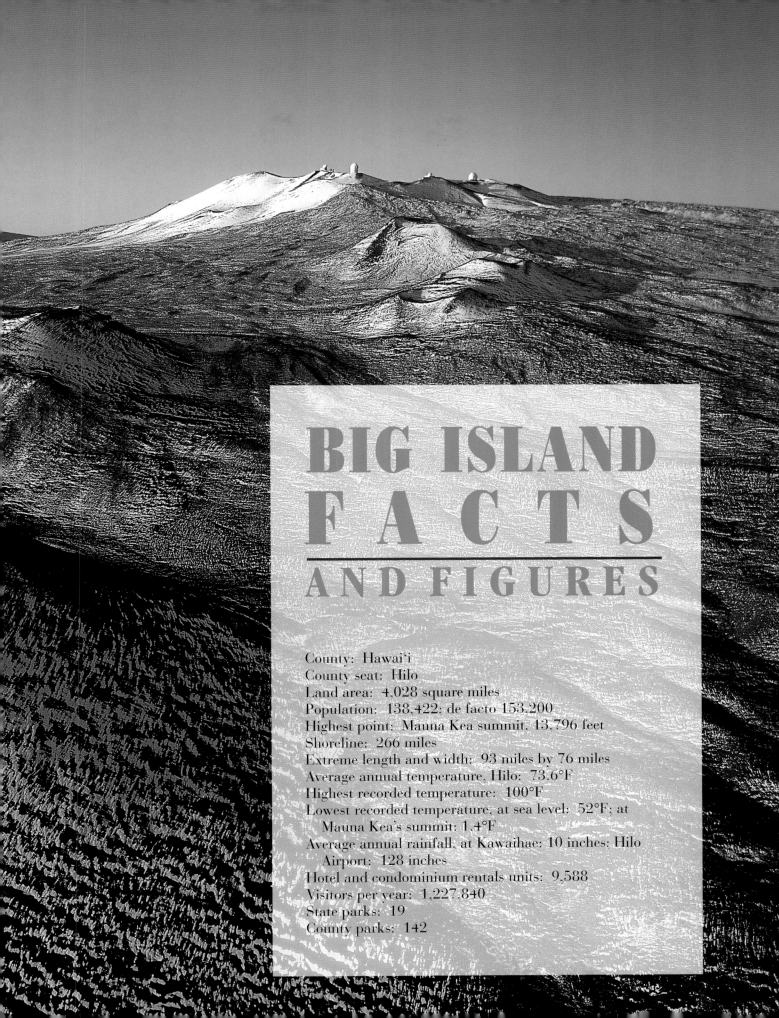

BIG ISLAND
FACTS
AND FIGURES

County: Hawai'i
County seat: Hilo
Land area: 4,028 square miles
Population: 138,422; de facto 153,200
Highest point: Mauna Kea summit, 13,796 feet
Shoreline: 266 miles
Extreme length and width: 93 miles by 76 miles
Average annual temperature, Hilo: 73.6°F
Highest recorded temperature: 100°F
Lowest recorded temperature, at sea level: 52°F; at
    Mauna Kea's summit: 1.4°F
Average annual rainfall, at Kawaihae: 10 inches; Hilo
    Airport: 128 inches
Hotel and condominium rentals units: 9,588
Visitors per year: 1,227,840
State parks: 19
County parks: 142

Just outside of Hilo, Akaka Falls drops 442 feet straight down. Protected and cared for by the Hawai'i State Park service, this cascade and plunge pool are surrounded by a rain forest of giant ginger, heliconia, ferns, orchids, and bamboo.

BIG ISLAND

The island of Hawai'i, commonly called by locals "the Big Island," is the youngest, broadest, and highest island in the chain. The expanse and sheer magnitude of this geologically alive landmass make every human structure—including the glitzy mega-resorts along the western shore—seem paltry by comparison.

The island comprises five shield volcanoes: Kohala, the oldest and most eroded; Hualalai; Mauna Kea, the highest; and the two active ones—mighty Mauna Loa, and its little sister Kilauea, which has been erupting for over fourteen years. Mauna Kea, if measured from its base on the ocean floor, is the tallest mountain in the world. These capacious peaks support varied landscapes, from parched black lava deserts to highland scrub to dense rain forests and alpine cloud forests.

During Hawai'i's recorded history (the last two centuries) more than a hundred major eruptions have reshaped the southern districts of the island, especially in Puna. The lava is part of the nonstop process that began a million years ago and that still builds the island. Rivers of molten rock burn towns, inundate the foundations, and leave behind only fresh fields of black stone. Beaches turn to cliffs and instant new beaches of surf-blown lava particles appear. A fire fountain deposits a new cinder cone. Earthquakes drop sections of coastline a foot or two. Roads close.

The Big Island shivers with life. A dynamic energy animates the whole landscape, whether it's actually bubbling with magma or not. It's hard to describe this living land adequately. It has to be felt.

Until recently the island enjoyed a sleepy anonymity, its economy based on sugar cane and ranching. Then the big resorts began sprouting up along the perpetually sunny leeward coast, the Kona airport expanded, and the volcanic wonderland became an international destination. Its quiet little towns have started to fuss about traffic lights. Suddenly it seems that the entire world is driving past the tiny post office, flashing cameras, and squinting at road maps.

Yet the new grand hotels, airports, roads, shopping centers, and warehouse districts are still dwarfed by all the outdoor grandeur. The overwhelming scale of the island—and the power it suggests—render everything else insignificant.

The Hawaiians understood this. Remnants of their life as it was before the *haoles* (foreigners; Caucasians) arrived are rather insubstantial: just a few trails, agricultural terraces, fishponds, walls, rock carvings (petroglyphs), shelter sites, and several large platforms of rock, called *heiau*. These stony ramparts were built atop hills or at strategic harbors or on advantageous fields. *Heiau* were places of worship and ritual, dedicated to fishing gods, gods of the fields, the great lizard gods (*moʻo*), war gods, and the ancestral gods of the great chiefs. Men, gods, and nature met at the stone altars to honor the sacred compacts which bound them inextricably and fearfully together. Those who study the history and culture of the Hawaiians invariably note the remarkable harmony with nature sustained by these muscular Polynesians, who used their unsurpassed seafaring arts to find Paradise.

They first landed at South Point, Ka Lae, on the Big Island about 1,500 years ago. Westerners, or what the Hawaiians politely called *haoles*, arrived in 1778, when Captain James Cook of His Majesty's Navy discovered Kauaʻi. A year later Cook's ships returned, anchoring at Kealakekua Bay, a few miles south of today's Kailua-Kona. The British captain was royally feted; but later he was clubbed to death in a scuffle, when some Hawaiians stole a ship's launch and caused a confrontation. A shooting incident followed. To shield themselves from British bullets, the Hawaiian villagers held up flimsy mats woven from the leaves of the *hala* tree.

One young chief who watched the brief barrage was Kamehameha, the Lonely One, who would later conquer the Big Island, Maui, and Oʻahu with the help of *haole* guns. He established the Kamehameha dynasty and the Kingdom of Hawaiʻi, which lasted over 100 years.

New England missionaries arrived at Kailua-Kona in 1819. Eight short decades later the Hawaiian Islands were annexed by the United States. During the intervening years, the Hawaiian population, ravaged by introduced diseases, declined from at least 300,000 to about 50,000.

By the time of annexation, the lands of Hawaiʻi had already shifted to private ownership and had been consolidated in huge *haole*-owned cattle ranches and sugar plantations. A small cattle herd left in Kohala

The broad, snowcapped dome of Mauna Kea, the "white mountain," towers over the heart of *paniolo* country.

by English captain George Vancouver as a gift for the chief Kamehameha became the nucleus for what is now the Parker Ranch and its impressive 225,000 acres of ranch land and 55,000 head of cattle.

The sugar plantation managers of the Hamakua and Kaʻu districts, in need of cheap and dependable labor, arranged for the immigration of foreign workers into Hawaiʻi to tend and harvest the profitable sugar fields. First, laborers came from China, then Portugal, Japan, Korea, Okinawa, and, finally, the Philippines. They did the backbreaking work, fulfilled their contracts, saved money, started families, and eventually moved from the plantation camps into towns or to Oʻahu.

Coffee groves in Kona, lettuce fields in Kamuela, macadamia orchards in Kaʻu, and cow pastures in Kohala give the Big Island relief from the endless plantation "lawns" that characterize the other islands. Diversified agriculture has allowed each of the island's far-flung rural communities to develop its own unique character.

Hilo, the Big Island's big town, had the airport, seaport, and easy access to Kilauea volcano, which had been set aside by the U.S. government in 1916 as Volcanoes National Park. Hilo was the logical place for an infant sightseeing industry, and a few hotels were built there in the early 1960s. But the rainy climate kept the visitor counts low, while Oʻahu and Maui's visitor industries boomed.

The old royal playground at Kona, on the drier leeward coast, had blue sky and history to give this area prestige. By the early 1970s, its sunny coastline was busy with low-rise condos, hotels, and pricey vacation homes. Keahole Airport near Kona began accepting flights directly from the mainland.

The big ranches sold huge oceanfront lava fields in South Kohala and North Kona to developers from the mainland and Japan, whose ambitions and financial resources were bigger than anything Hawaiʻi had ever seen. The resort boom was on.

One landowner who didn't have to sell was the Bishop Estate, the fee-holder to hundreds of thousands of acres on Hawaiʻi, Maui, and Oʻahu. Hawaiʻi's largest

Helmeted cyclists on bike tours are a common site along the roads of the Kohala Coast.

Kauna'oa Beach, within the Mauna Kea Beach Resort in South Kohala, lies about a mile south of Kawaihae on Queen Ka'ahumanu Highway.

Mo'okini Heiau, in North Kohala, was constructed around 480 A.D. The grass hut housed the *kahu*, or caretaker of the *heiau*.

Lapakahi is a partially restored Hawaiian fishing village dating back to the fourteenth century. Paths, low rock walls of the old dwellings, and specimen trees and plants used by the Hawaiians are the only signs of a vanished way of life.

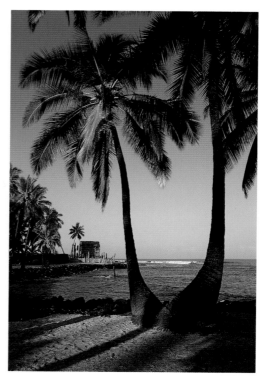

The reconstructed heiau and Hale o Keawe mausoleum at Pu'uhonua o Honaunau (Place of Refuge) stand as monuments to the complex social structure that governed the lives of the ancient Hawaiians.

47

private landholder, Bishop Estate is the legacy of the Kamehameha dynasty, held in perpetual trust for the education and general benefit of Hawaiian children. It has developed a multi-hotel golf resort at Keauhou on lands where the warrior-king Kamehameha I once lived.

It is not certain when Kamehameha was born, because dates were not accurately kept by the Hawaiian oral historians. Scholars assume it was in the 1750s, in Kohala at 'Upolu Point, where the supposed birthing site has been sensitively preserved.

As a boy, Kamehameha learned modern warfare and modern commerce and took advantage of both. He forged the Hawaiian nation from a group of warring chiefdoms and made it prosperous according to the European definition of prosperity. When he died in Kona in 1819 at his compound at Kailua Bay, where the King Kamehameha Hotel now stands, he was an old man still praying to his gods.

The life and legend of Kamehameha pervade the Big Island even today. The touchstones of the island's history and lore are his birthplace at 'Upolu Point, his great war *heiau* at Pu'ukohola, his lands at Keauhou, the fishponds at 'Anaeho'omalu, his refuge at Waipi'o, and the site of his death on the shores of Kailua Bay. After his passing, Kamehameha's sacred bones, thought to be the vessels for his immortal spirit, were carried away to a secret burial cave. Although many fortune hunters have searched for this greatest tomb of Hawai'i's royalty, the cave has never been found.

The coarse, icy snow of Mauna Kea is a challenge for even the most expert snowman artist. This man, made with the rarely used "pack and slap" technique, won't last long in the tropical sun, even at these elevations.

A lonely *paniolo* from Kamuela heads home through the green hills and fertile pastures of Parker Ranch, the largest cattle ranch in America.

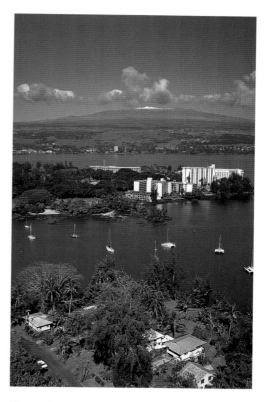

The calm waters of Reed's Bay in Hilo, one of the most expansive natural harbors in Hawai'i, make it very popular with yachting enthusiasts.

Lili'uokalani Garden, a Japanese-style park complete with ponds, pagodas, and bridges, is the largest formal oriental garden outside of Japan.

49

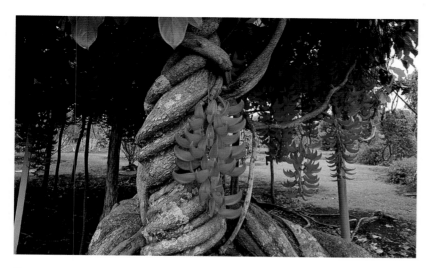

This hanging red jade vine is just one of the many rare and exotic specimens of flora found at the Nani Mau Botanical Gardens.

Named for the constant iridescence that appears in the sunlit cascading water, Rainbow Falls feeds the Wailuku River just outside of Hilo.

The gullied terrain of the Haumakua Coast, north of Hilo, was once covered with fields of sugar cane. Now the rolling plains and sheer ravines are known as "the macadamia nut capital of Hawai'i."

Hiking clearly marked trails through the rain forests of the Hawai'i Volcanoes National Park is a wonderful way to see tree ferns and *'ohi'a*.

Fiery orange and ash black in summer, the cinder cones at the summit of Mauna Kea soften in winter beneath white blankets of pure, high-altitude snow.

Like a scene of pre-historic majesty, the dramatic coastline near Pololu in North Kohala has the rugged power of new earth.

The magnificently clear waters of Kealakekua Bay are perfect for viewing the young reefs that have formed over submerged lava flows.

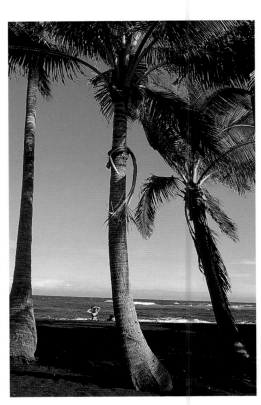

The black sands at Punalu'u beach in the South Point district are the result of Pele's mad rush to the sea.

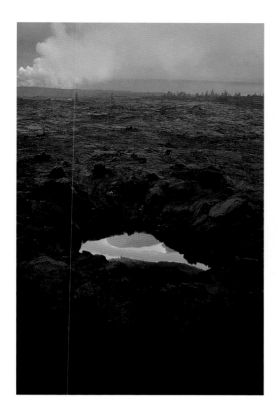

This view into a lava tube through a collapsed "skylight" shows a river of 2,000-degree lava.

The southeastern flank of Kilauea Volcano erupted on January 3, 1983 with spectacular lava fountains shooting into the sky. Though not always so dramatic, the current phase of volcanic activity has lasted over 14 years.

The rugged Puna Coast, still raw with young lava, simmers in the golden light of the setting sun.

Fire and water collide in dramatic roars, hisses, and plumes of smoke as Pele, the volcano goddess, pushes new land into the sea.

Rivulets of gleaming lava converge on their journey from Kilauea Volcano to the sea.

Pleasure yachts and commercial sightseeing vessels dot the deep blue waters off the historic town of Lahaina. Located on the western coast of the island of Maui, this quaint little town, now a renowned tourist destination, once boiled with excitement as the center of the whaling industry of the Pacific

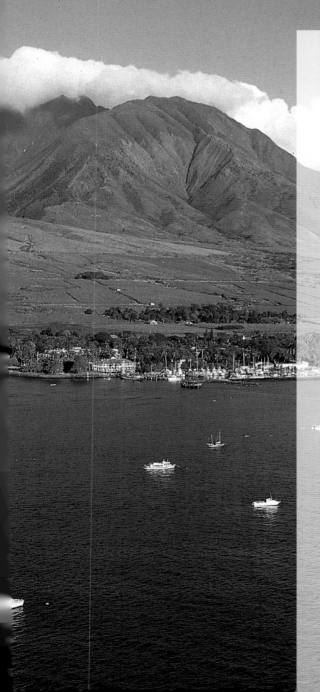

MAUI
FACTS
AND FIGURES

County: Maui, which includes the islands of Maui,
   Molokaʻi, Lanaʻi, and Kahoʻolawe
County seat: Wailuku
Land area: 727 square miles
Population: 117,100; de facto, 156,400. Third most
   populous county in state.
Highest point: Puʻuʻulaʻula (Red Hill), Haleakala,
   10,023 feet
Shoreline: 120 miles
Extreme length and width: 48 miles by 26 miles
Average annual temperature: 75.5°F
Highest recorded temperature: 98°F
Lowest recorded temperature (at sea level): 48°F; at
   Haleakala's summit: 14°F
Average annual rainfall: Kihei: 13 inches
Average annual rainfall: Puʻu Kukui, West Maui
   Mountains 300 plus inches
Hotel and condominium rental units: 17,824 (1996)
Visitors per year: 2,327,220
National parks: 2
State parks: 13
County parks: 102

A line of cupped cinder cones crosses the desolate interior of Haleakala Valley. Many have compared this barren view to the surface of the moon. At sunrise, the sun god La puts on a spectacular show for those adventurous souls who brave the cold and pre-dawn darkness.

M A U I

The island of Maui gets its name from the muscular Polynesian trickster Maui the demigod, who is credited in legend with fishing up the entire chain of the Hawaiian Islands with a magical fish hook. He also climbed to the top of the island's mighty volcano—Haleakala, the "House of the Sun"—and pushed the sky high into the heavens so people could walk upright, and run and jump without fear of knocking their heads on the sky god's belly.

That mythical dynamism is central to the island that bears Maui's name, and plays itself out daily in the robust activities of residents and tourists alike. A certain freedom pervades the magical atmosphere of this high-sky place, and everyone revels in its unmatched venues for windsurfing, mountain hiking, snorkeling, cycling, sailing, and plain lying out in the Maui sunshine.

The second largest of the Islands, Maui is dominated by Haleakala, rising 10,023 feet above sea level, and the older West Maui Mountains, at a maximum height of 5,778 feet at the top of Pu'u Kukui. The isthmus between the two volcanic peaks supports most of Maui's growing population and its waning sugar cane industry. The county seat, Wailuku, on the northern end of the isthmus, is joined by its sister town Kahului, site of the island's deep-water port and an airport that accepts direct flights from the U.S. mainland.

Offshore are four junior islands, all part of Maui County. Sleepy Moloka'i struggles to maintain its rural character. Lana'i was recently transformed from a pineapple plantation to an exclusive private resort. Kaho'olawe was a U.S. Navy bombing target for many years. And Molokini, a tiny crescent-shaped volcanic cone, is very popular as a snorkeling destination.

Together with the Big Island of Hawai'i, Maui was the stage for ancient Hawai'i's most important events and wars. An era of peace between the rival chiefs of Maui and Hawai'i gave way in the 1600s to two centuries of endless bloodshed. The Maui dynasty of Kekaulike and his son Kahekili was finally defeated in 1790 by the powerful chief from the Big Island, Kamehameha the Conqueror.

By 1802, Kamehameha had unified all the Hawaiian Islands except Kaua'i (which he obtained peacefully in 1810). As the first king of a united Hawai'i, he established his royal capital at Lahaina on Maui's leeward coast.

To show his respect for the superior Maui bloodlines, and to secure those bloodlines for his royal heirs, Kamehameha married two of Maui's most chiefly women: Ka'ahumanu and the sacred princess Ke'opuolani. After his death, his Maui queens retired the old Hawaiian gods and, at the urging of their Protestant missionary advisors, led the Hawaiian conversion to Christianity. Heiau, the simple stone temples of Hawaiian worship, were torn down and replaced by churches and schools, where texts printed in the Hawaiian language taught spiritual and practical learning.

Whales put Maui on the map 150 years ago, when whalers from the eastern U.S. and Europe used the safe and convenient anchorage at Lahaina for a central provisioning stop in the whale-rich northern Pacific. As many as 400 ships dropped anchor there every year during the 1840s. Grog shops and lawlessness proliferated, along with commerce and growth. At the time, Lahaina's native and foreign population was about 3,500 people and 528 dogs.

The discovery of petroleum in Pennsylvania in 1871 put an abrupt end to the whale oil business and the whaling fleets. The royal seat of the kingdom was moved to the larger commercial port at Honolulu on O'ahu. Lahaina was all but deserted.

For the next century, Maui slumbered as its vast lands were consolidated into sugar cane and pineapple plantations, and its mountain streams were tapped for irrigation water. Until the early 1960s, Maui was little more than a few plantation camps, cattle ranches, isolated fishing villages, a half-dozen Spartan hotels,

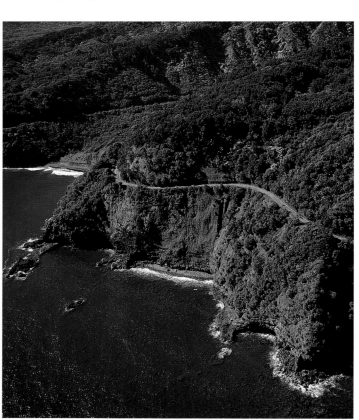

The winding switch-backs and hairpin curves on the road to Hana have helped maintain the area's quaint ambiance. Many a traveler has lost a breakfast or lunch alongside this swerving, turning byway.

and plenty of space. The sugar fields spread uninterrupted like rich lawns from the foot of the mountains to the beaches.

The tourist boom began at Ka'anapali in 1962. For the next 25 years and continuing today, resort hotels, golf courses, and vacation condominiums have seemed to sprout wherever there is a sunny swimming beach. Little Kahului airport, long accustomed to a few inter-island flights daily, found itself welcoming nonstop jumbo jets direct from mainland U.S. cities.

At the same time, mainland hippies found the deeper meaning of "mellow" on Maui's remote beaches and in the smoky haze of its famous *pakalolo* (marijuana). The island became a world-renowned playground for the Age of Aquarius.

The current Maui lifestyle now attracts large numbers of "life-stylists" to the island's seaside condominiums and chic Upcountry cabins. These folk settle down for a few years as realtors, hotel bartenders, carpenters, small shop owners, and trust-fund windsurfers. As a result, Maui is the fastest growing and most heavily *haole* (Caucasian) of all the islands.

About two-and-a-half million visitors now spend $1.5 billion on Maui each year. On an average day, 42,000 visitors share the island with a resident population that has passed the 100,000 mark. Locals grumble about traffic that most newcomers barely notice.

Amid all the glitzy resorts and swank restaurants, Maui manages to keep its island character and its soaring beauty alive. To be enjoyed are its natural and man-made wonders, its country roads, ancient temples, peaceful beaches, blazing sunsets, misty rains, friendly smiles, and dewy flowers.

South of Hana, near the end of the paved road, are the Pools of 'Ohe'o. A series of small waterfalls links the pools in a natural watery stairway from the mountain to the sea.

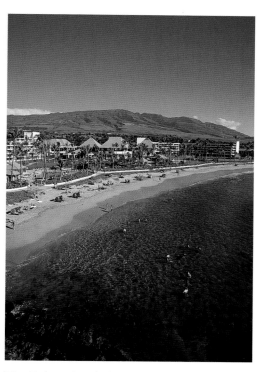

The Polynesian-style peaked roof lines of the Sheraton Maui grace the shore of the west-facing beach at Ka'anapali.

Upcountry Maui, home to proud *paniolos*, or Hawaiian cowboys, has the feel of Montana with a tropical twist.

A golden sunrise outlines the ragged contours of 'Alau Island off the coast of Hana.

Storm-fed waterfalls pound into hidden plunge pools along the windward cliffs of Haleakala between Kipahulu and Kaupo.

The public beach park at Fleming Beach was named for David
Thomas Fleming, the early manager of Honolua Ranch and

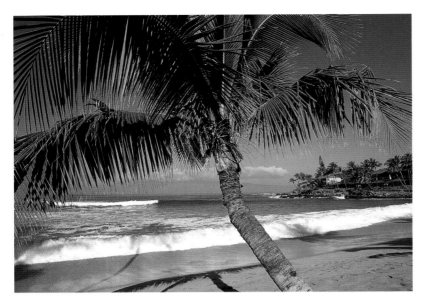

The roaring surf and sandy, white beach of Napili Bay, near Kipahulu, make this a popular swimming spot for visitors and locals.

For 200 years of Island history Lahaina Harbor was a major port and royal playground. Today, the harbor is home to fishing, tour, and pleasure boats that continue the rich tradition.

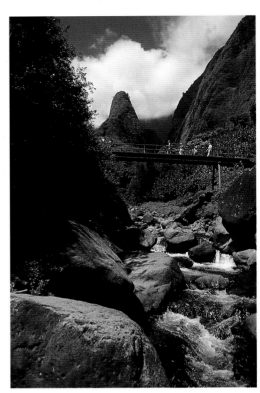

'Iao Needle, located in the West Maui Mountains, was the site where Kamehameha the Great defeated the armies of Maui's chief Kalanikupule.

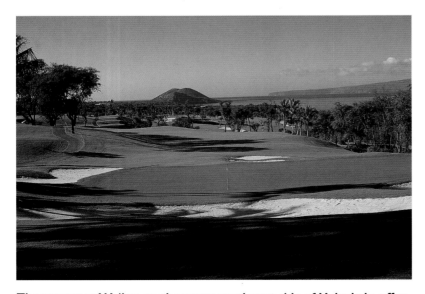

The resorts at Wailea, on the sunny southwest side of Haleakala, offer grand hotels, condominiums, and world-class golf courses.

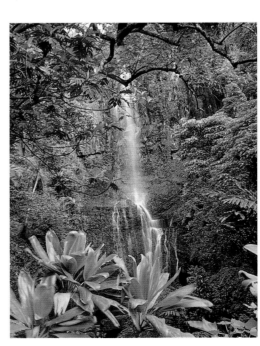

Wailua Falls, on the Hana Highway just before the Seven Pools of Kipahulu, is an archetypal vision of paradise.

Once hunted in Hawai'i's coastal waters, the gentle humpback whales now breach and play with their newborn calves in the 'Au'au Channel off Lahaina.

At Kapalua the paved Honoapi'ilani Highway ends. Off shore, silhouetted by the setting sun, is the island of Moloka'i.

The half-submerged crater, Molokini Islet, is a major feature of South Maui.

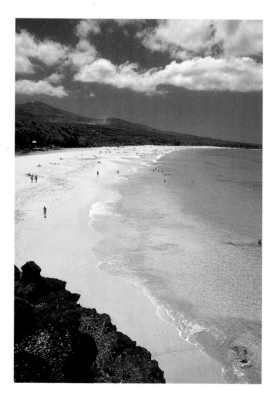

The broad white sand and glistening blue water of Makena Beach in South Maui make this a local favorite.

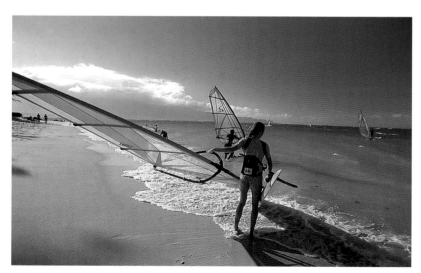

Maui's unique wind and sea conditions are perfect for the sport of windsurfing.

The stunning green ridges and dramatic cliffs of the northern coast of Moloka'i catch the trade-wind rains and selfishly hoard the cool water. Shaped like a manō (shark), this island is home to Hawai'i's most culturally-connected Hawaiians.

FACTS
AND FIGURES

KAHO'OLAWE

Land area: Kaho'olawe 44.6 square miles
Population: uninhabited
Highest point: Pu'u Moaulanui, 1,483 feet
Extreme length and width: 11 miles by 6 miles

LANA'I

Land area: Lana'i, 140.5 square miles
Population: 2,989 (1995)
Highest point: Lanaihale, 3,366 feet
Extreme length and width: 18 miles by 13 miles

MOLOKA'I

Land area: Moloka'i, 260 square miles;
Population: 6,838 (1995)
Highest point: Kamakou, 4,961 feet
Extreme length and width: 38 miles by 10 miles

A 45-minute jeep ride over unimproved roads transports visitors from the tropical scenery of the Saddle Road to the high-mountain snows of Mauna Kea. The summit of this great mountain offers the remarkably thin, clear air that astronomers find ideal for star gazing.

KAHO'OLAWE

Sheltered by the vast bulk of nearby Haleakala from Hawai'i's moisture-laden northeast trade winds, low-lying Kaho'olawe is now barren red "hardpan," impenetrable to rain or roots. Kaho'olawe translates as "the carrying away," and the island has indeed been carried away in a 200-year plume of fine red dust.

Inhabited only intermittently in ancient times by fishermen, star-wise navigators, and gatherers of fine-grained basalt and obsidian (for spear points), Kaho'olawe enjoyed a brief commercial career in the 1930s as an offshore annex to Maui's Haleakala and 'Ulupalakua ranches. But with the approach of World War II, civilian access was curtailed and from 1940 to 1995 the island absorbed millions of rounds of U.S. and Allied naval and aircraft gunfire. It had become a target island for war games. Hawaiian activists succeed in getting the Navy to give Kaho'olawe back to the state as a cultural sanctuary, but only after decades of dramatic protests.

While it has rarely been prominent commercially, Kaho'olawe often has been useful. Pre-Cook navigators supposedly used the island landmarks as guides for starting the long voyage back to Tahiti, and nineteenth century opium runners found the deserted island handy. Their legacy today is a sandy "Smugglers' Cove."

The tiny island of Kaho'olawe, a desert environ trapped in the rain-shadow of Maui's Haleakala, once served as the ancient Hawaiian navigational landmark at the open-ocean entry to the island chain. In the post World War II years this 11 mile long remnant of an old volcano was used as a bombing target by the United States Navy. Today, Kaho'olawe's virgin coves and reefs are a favorite landing point for pleasure cruises and snorkeling expeditions launched from the Maui ports of Lahaina and Ma'alaea.

Shipwreck Beach, a long stretch of wind-blown white sand on the north coast of Lana'i, acquired its name during the late 1800s and early 1900s when wooden sailing ships and steamers ran aground on the offshore reefs.

LANA'I

One of the two "dry" islands lying in the rain shadow of Maui's immense Haleakala (uninhabited Kaho'olawe is the other), Lana'i attracted few settlements in ancient times. Wary of the *'uhane* (ghosts) and *akua* (fierce gods) which dwelt there, sensible Hawaiians avoided arid Lana'i for cooler, moister Maui, Moloka'i, and O'ahu.

Pineapple planter James Dole laid the foundation for today's Lana'i when he plowed his first pineapple fields at Wahiawa, outside Honolulu, in 1901 and founded Hawai'i's first successful canning operation. Subsequently, his Dole Corporation purchased 98 percent of Lana'i island from the Territorial government. The remaining two percent is in pie-shaped land divisions owned by long-time Hawaiian families.

With a population of 2,400, largely descendants of Filipino, Portuguese, and Japanese immigrant workers, Lana'i City, the lone community, remains the state's foremost "company town," although many families long ago bought their own homes and businesses from Castle & Cooke, corporate owners of Dole. Until very recently, the community of lofty pines and tidy cottages was so quiet you could trace the progress of a jeep or pickup through Lana'i City by the sequential barking of dogs. But the late 80s brought changes when the pineapple plantation closed and two world-class resorts opened, one upland in Ko'ele, and the other at Manele Bay.

Like their neighbors across the channel on Moloka'i, Lana'i folks are known for their hunting and fishing skills, their self-sufficiency, their generosity, and their love of family and community. The island is famed for its forested uplands, empty wind-swept beaches, and the stark sea cliffs along the western shore, at the foot of which are some of Hawai'i's best fishing and diving.

The Ko'ele Lodge, one of Lana'i's exclusive resorts, is nestled on an upland plateau that was once covered with a patchwork of pineapple fields.

The petroglyph field at Luahiwa is one of the sites where ancient Hawaiians left pictorial history etched into lava rock faces.

Kalaupapa Peninsula was formed by a small shield volcano whose lava flow fanned into a flat, leaf-shaped land mass near the center of the northern coast of Moloka'i. During the leprosy epedemic of the mid to late 1800s, many of Hawai'i's oriental and Hawaiian community were quarantined on this spit of isolated land. Today, the Kalaupapa settlement is designated as a National Park. The only land access to the park is down the 26 winding switchbacks along the cliff-side trail that has always served as Kalaupapa's link with the

MOLOKA'I

Although its size and mountainous terrain would seemingly lump Moloka'i with the big islands of Hawai'i, Maui, O'ahu, and Kaua'i, the island's rural values and the survival skills of its residents bespeak a closer kinship with Lana'i and Ni'ihau. With an economy that has been moribund for decades, Moloka'i produces more than its share of hunters, fishermen, and farmers.

It also has the state's most prominent ethnic Hawaiian community, due in part to the substantial Hawaiian Homestead acreage at Ho'olehua. Of Moloka'i's seven thousand residents, about five thousand classify themselves as Hawaiian or part-Hawaiian, a ratio exceeded only on tiny Ni'ihau. Farming, fishing, and tourism are the principal dollar earners.

Two great ranches dominate the island—arid Moloka'i Ranch on the western half, and rainy *Pu'u o Hoku* ("hill of stars") Ranch in the east. In between are mile-high mountains, vast inaccessible valleys, and some of Hawai'i's broadest reefs. Locked up for years by Moloka'i Ranch, the splendid coves and beaches of Moloka'i's West End were finally opened to the public late in the 1970s with the development of the Kaluako'i Resort near three-mile-long Papohaku Beach.

On the island's wild and spectacular north shore opposite Kaunakakai is the famous Kalaupapa settlement where Father Damien de Veuster spent his last years administering to Hawai'i's neglected nineteenth century leprosy patients. Situated on a low peninsula guarded by some of the world's loftiest sea cliffs, Kalaupapa is a unique and soul-stirring community.

Hawai'i's nearly extinct flora is protected at the Kamakou Preserve near the peak of Moloka'i's east volcano.

Constructed in 1873, St. Philomena Church has come to represent Father Joseph Damien de Veuster's humanitarian work with the leper patients of Kalaupapa.

Moaʻula Falls tumbles through the lush green depths of Halawa Valley on the northeastern tip of island of Molokaʻi.

Planted by King Kamehameha V in the 1860s, the Kapuaiwa Coconut Grove once covered ten acres and contained over 1,000 trees.

Steep seacliffs, sand dunes, a fresh water pool, and a rugged beach make up the dramatic Moʻomomi Preserve on Molokaʻi's northeastern shore.

For many years this string of patient mules was the only transportation to and from the isolated community of Kalaupapa. Laboriously, these plodding caravans transported cargo down the steep and winding cliff-trail to the leper colony below.

The Sheraton-Molokaʻi, one of the island's luxury resorts, is perched on the northwestern tip of Kepuhi Bay. On a clear night the lights of Oʻahu can be seen from Kepuhi Beach.